ABC's of Leadership

26 Characteristics of more effective Leadership

David M. Hall

Bloomington, IN Milton Keynes, UK
authorHOUSE®

AuthorHouse™
1663 Liberty Drive, Suite 200
Bloomington, IN 47403
www.authorhouse.com
Phone: 1-800-839-8640

AuthorHouse™ UK Ltd.
500 Avebury Boulevard
Central Milton Keynes, MK9 2BE
www.authorhouse.co.uk
Phone: 08001974150

First published by AuthorHouse 3/26/2007

ISBN: 978-1-4259-6967-7 (sc)

Library of Congress Control Number: 2006909258

Printed in the United States of America
Bloomington, Indiana

This book is printed on acid-free paper.

This book is dedicated to the memory of

Glen David Hall

The author acknowledges the encouragement and assistance of:

Gary D. Hall

Jacqueline V. Hall

Dr. Louis Firenze

and many others who encouraged this publication.

Introduction

Are you a leader? Who would want to follow you? Why? These are some questions each of us should ask ourselves before deciding that we have the ability and capability to be a leader.

Are you a leader? We all have some leadership traits and capabilities. This alone does not make us a leader. First, we need many traits. We also need the ability to apply these traits in a fair and equitable manner. Good leaders also have a desire to lead. Desire alone is not enough. Desire without capability is a disaster about to happen.

Who would want to follow you? People who do not wish to be leaders would probably follow you. This gives them the ability to get things done without being responsible for the success or failure of the task or project. An additional category of people who may want to follow you are people who feel they can learn from you. These people usually find a way to move on after they have learned as much as they feel they can from you, their leader. They may even want your job.

There has been great discussion through the years about whether leadership and management are the same or if there is a significant enough difference for leadership to be a field of study all on its own.

The answer is obvious to those who understand leadership. When one considers the large contingent of managers who do not understand the difference between leadership and management, it is clear that more needs to be done to educate the managers and leaders in our corporations and non-profit organizations.

A review of this book will reveal thoughts from many sources. Many of these sources have been lost through the years that I have been engaged in the leadership process. These ideas have been helpful to me in my quest to be a better leader and a positive influence in the lives of the people with whom I have had the pleasure of working.

I pass them on to you in the hope that they will make you an even better leader.

Enjoy.

Table of Contents

I

Adversity

"Overcoming adversity requires resolve." Author unknown

In the tenth grade, my son tried out for the basketball team at his high school. The process followed a standard procedure that the coach had used apparently, for years. The first step in the process was an interview after the student had declared an interest in playing on the team. Next the coach would observe the student on the court. As a result of this step, the coach would garner a feel for what position the student had potential.

If you were not cut at this point, you then competed for a starting berth on the team. Once the starting team was selected, others were to be back-up to various positions in event they were needed during a game. In other words, they were the bench. Since a good bench is important, these players are also tasked to be as close to the starting five, in expertise, as possible. Thus the team and the back-up were selected.

My son was cut. This was devastating to him. He had worked hard to earn a starting berth on the team. In addition he felt that he was a better player than the person selected as starter and as back-up for the forward position for which he competed. In addition, some of his teammates felt, as he did, that the starter was not that good. The teammates voiced, to my son, he was a better player.

Now this is a dilemma. He approached the coach. The coach was unrelenting in his decision to eliminate him. No appeal or approach worked. The coach had made up his mind and the decision was final.

Somewhat dejected and now frustrated from discussions with the coach, but encouraged by the good words of his teammates, he started home. He found me in the family room. As he approached me his tirade began. He allowed that he was the better player of the two starting forwards. He even assured me that this was not his assessment alone. He had the assurances of many of his teammates that he was not just better but much better.

I listened intently. It was clear that he was disturbed. This age is a difficult time in the life of a teenager. He did not need me to add to his worries. Out of the blue, a thought came to me and I responded to him without hesitation. "Son!" I said. "You have two choices. You can be a victim and feel sorry for yourself, or you can go out there and prove the coach wrong!"

It was clear to me that was not the answer he was looking for. He retreated to his room without another word, and we did not further discuss his experience with the basketball team.

I am pleased though that he took his position on the second team seriously. He did so well on the second team that he was again recommended for the first team. In effect, he did go out there and prove the coach wrong. He made the team. He did well. Actually, at one point he had a shooting average of 100%. During that short (very short but impressive) period, he made every shot he attempted.

We are in charge of ourselves. If we want the results to be different, we need to do something different. In changing ourselves, we have a better opportunity to change others through our influence and example. Things will not always go the way we want. Things will not always be fair, but it is up to us to deal with the issues by proving our own merit, rather than finding fault with others.

> *"You can't solve a problem with the same*
> *mentality that created it."* Anonymous

II

Brave

"Every one is born into the world to do something unique and something distinctive and if he or she does not do it, it will never be done." Benjamin E. Mays

Being brave is not an easy task. It suggests that a leader is willing to face the difficulty of the organization. This could cause pain and suffering to a leader's career. No one is interested in pain and suffering, but someone has to do it.

In this day and age when every organization is trying to cut costs in an effort to be more competitive, leaders must be brave. A leader is brave when one of his people makes a mistake that costs the company serious money and the leader takes responsibility for the mistake. Mistakes can sometimes get the attention of everyone at the highest levels of the organization. This could leave the reputation of the leader in question. In the past, leaders and managers have found someone to blame. Actually the manager/leader should take the responsibility for the error, the excess cost or the cost overrun.

A night shift operator in the computer room made a mistake in the processing. This caused the reports, delivered to the customer, to be wrong. When the supervisor was approached, he made every effort to blame the mistake on the system. When it became obvious that a name was essential, he gave one with great reluctance. The supervisor was then in shock when he was told that the mistake was really his fault because people don't make mistakes on purpose. They are made because they have inadequate training or an incomplete set of tools to do the job. The leader insisted that the supervisor take the responsibility and be brave in view of the difficulty involved.

People should also be brave enough to tell their leader that the decision they have made is not a good one. Too often people feel that the leader wants someone to agree with them. Nothing is further from the truth. Leaders need people who will assess their decisions and the impact it will have on the people and the operation and keep the leader advised. After all, the supervisor is closer to the issues than the top management people.

Some leaders do not take bad news well. They sometimes react with anger, disappointment, frustration and a host of other attitudes. In effect, their real feelings come through in their actions.

A friend of mine tells the story of giving his boss some bad news. The leader remonstrated angrily and even used a few four letter invectives. It was so bad that the friend returned to his office and suggested to his people that they needed to be prepared to manage the operation without him. He felt the anger was so bad that surely he would be fired. While in the process of explaining what happened, the telephone rang. It was the leader. With a calmness that was shocking, in view of his anger a few minutes earlier, he said, "I just had a thought that may resolve our problem. Come on up to the office and let's discuss it."

All things cannot go smoothly all the time. There will be times when the leader must be aware of difficult times or when the train has run off the track. Killing the messenger with anger and invectives, does not help the situation. Leaders must learn how to accept the good, bad and ugly with dignity and without revealing extreme feelings.

Leaders must gain control of their organization and remain in control. Losing ones temper is a way of losing control. Keep calm and poised at all times. Our people will disappoint us periodically. We must insure that the worker learns from the mistakes and have established a mechanism to prevent a repeat of the same mistake. A worker can only do this in an environment where honesty is appreciated and applauded. When this environment is created, not only will you have the proper information, you will have a workforce that will help you with a fix through ideas and execution. In the language of the teenagers of today, "Be cool!"

> *"It is easy to be ordinary, but it takes real courage to excel." Eddie Finnigan*

III

Caring

"People don't care how much you know until they know how much you care." Anonymous

"I don't know and I don't care." This was the response to the question, "When it comes to youth, what do you think of their low voting percentage?" It is all right not to care what people think about certain issues that do not interest you. When it comes to the people in the business organization, it is important to show each person that you, the leader, cares.

We spend much of our time, in the workplace, impressing people with our superior knowledge of the products and/or services, the company and the industry. Whereas this is important, it pales in comparison to impress people with the thought that you care – about them. Some wise philosopher once said, "People don't care how much you know until they know how much you care!"

How do you show a person you care? There are several ways. One very important way is to treat a person with dignity and respect. "Thanks" and "Please" go a long way in getting people to do your bidding and convincing them that you have their best interests at heart. Too often we get in a hurry and forget to use these two important words. The more you use them the more your people will be endeared to you.

Another word important to showing you care is to use the term "we." No one accomplishes by himself/herself. If we did, we would not need co-workers or subordinates. Good leaders only use "I" when things have gone awry and they are taking full responsibility for what happened. W. Edwards Deming in his book *Out of the Crisis,* says, *". . . . missing in school is the teaching of civic responsibilities in the form of a system for win, win."* It is important that we insure that others do not lose because of our actions. This shows a lack of concern and causes one to feel negatively about the leader and the organization.

When we are tasked with nurturing a baby we take full control and insure that the baby has what it needs to survive, grow and learn. We should nurture our employees and associates the same way. Nurturing includes, but is not limited to, taking care of, making changes that will positively impact the child, showing them how to do things that will show growth, and attempting to create a happy and positive environment. Should we do less for our subordinates? Certainly not! We should do these things for the people for whom we are responsible? Do not look at the people as if they were babies. This would be demeaning. Look at them as the adults that they are and give them the nurturing they deserve.

Perhaps, the greatest way we can show we care is to listen. Listening is the one form of communications that is seldom taught in the public schools. In an assemblage of students, less than one percent had ever had a course in listening. Those who had completed such a course indicated that the course was provided by their employer. Businesses have learned the importance of listening to the customer, the employee and the supplier. These are the people that help us to be a success in the marketplace. Thus, they are beginning to teach their people how to listen to these three constituents. Learning to listen can do wonders for showing people we leaders care.

Most successful people had a mentor at some point in their work life. Mentoring is the process of helping a person become "all that they can be," to use the U. S. Army motto. We must adopt a person, with potential, in the workplace and assist that person, as you were assisted, to understand the workplace and the culture of your organization. Some mentors prefer to work through someone else. The important thing is they are helping someone, with potential, to be successful.

Caring, then, is the hallmark of a successful relationship. Caring is also essential to influencing someone to consider something different. Caring is the key to success of both the leader and the manager and the subordinate. We can show that care by the words we use, the mentoring we provide and the listening that we do.

> *"Those who show care and concern for their fellowman*
> *have more power and influence than others."*
> *David M. Hall*

IV

Dealing with Difficult People

"The truth is that there is nothing noble in being superior to somebody else. The only real nobility is in being superior to your former self." ~Whitney Young

There you are, obeying the speed limit, traveling down the interstate, minding your own business and in love with the world, when someone cuts you off. This is one of the many things that can happen by people who seem uncaring and are difficult. Imagine a sister-in-law who enters your conversation and changes the subject. What do you do with a mother-in-law who continues to cast negative aspersions toward you at every opportunity? There are many other situations and types of difficult people that we have to deal with from day to day. The question is: How do we deal with them? Here are a few things that can help.

1. Analyze yourself. In each instance, if you analyze yourself, the person is difficult because you had other expectations. You didn't expect to have a car cut you off causing you to slam on your brakes. You expected your sister-in-law to at least say "excuse me" upon interrupting your conversation with someone else. Certainly you felt that your mother-in-law would be kinder to the person who is taking care of her daughter or son. We must abandon these expectations. Difficult people have no appreciation for how others feel. In addition they are not likely to feel the need to apologize. Understanding this you begin to expect them to not do things in a conventional way. Once you have abandoned these expectations you can begin to confront them.

2. Confront the difficult person. Make the person aware that you have no affinity for his/her rudeness. When you enter in discussions with the person you must be upfront, blunt and candid. If you use a soft approach to avoid hurting the person's feelings, the person will probably not listen and respond with further insults. The person may even decide they are the victim. Many difficult people are in denial. Many times difficult people speak in harsh tones to others but become insulted when someone speaks to them in the same tone of voice. Confrontation can cause conflict. The conflict must be endured if the person is to change his/her behavior. The sooner you have the conflict and resolve the issue, the more likely you are to have a harmonious relationship with the person. At first offense let it be known that you are not enchanted with his/her approach. An approach may be to say, "I beg your pardon. Am I to understand that you are "dissing" me? Is that what you meant to do?" This confrontation is not offensive and can draw attention to what the person did to offend you.

3. Attack the action. It is essential that you attack what is being done and not attack the person. Too often conflict is caused by correcting a person or complaining about a person. Let us leave the person whole and attack what the person has done. Another approach that can be used is to tell the difficult person how you feel when he/she becomes difficult. "Your behavior makes me feel that you do not care! I would appreciate it if you would not engage in that behavior." (The behavior should be identified.) People tend to be more accepting of someone disagreeing with what they have done rather than being attacked.

4. Build a relationship. Last, but not least, recognize that you are not going to change established behavior in one confrontation. Do not have great expectations after the first confrontation. It is hoped that you will have their attention. Keep that attention by working with the person, if they will permit, in a one-on-

one communication that can help you build a relationship with that person.

These steps are not all inclusive, but they can get you off to a good start in building a relationship with a difficult person. You must be patient. You must be understanding. You must not accept denial from the difficult person. Above all, you should not accept his/her disrespect.

"Adversity has the effect of eliciting talents which, in prosperous circumstances, would have lain dormant." -
- Horace

V

Encouragement

"Be Encouraged." Desmon Daniel

"You can do it!" Most of us have heard that sometime in our life. It was a bit of encouragement to keep me going at whatever the task. From time to time all of us need encouragement.

The things that we do can be encouraging to others. When my sons were young, I would try to teach them different things. Each of them learned how to make certain repairs on an automobile. They also learned some of the things to look for when driving a car to determine if certain problems existed. Each time one of them brought to my attention something that I had taught them or accomplished something I had shown them how to do, I was encouraged. I was encouraged because they had learned. Being me, I wanted to insure that they were ahead of their peers in whatever knowledge I could give them. It was always encouraging to know that they were ready for the next lesson.

When they saw my glee at their accomplishments they were encouraged. Being encouraged, they were ready for the next lesson. Without that encouragement from me and others, they would have less desire to accomplish. They were also encouraged because their peers looked on with awe when they could do things their friends could not. This gave them encouragement to learn even more.

Words can be encouraging. "Thank you", are two words of encouragement. Thank you shows appreciation. People like to be appreciated. "Press on!" "Give it a try!" These are just a couple of expressions that give people encouragement. There are many, many more. How you say it can also be important. If you don't mean it don't say it. People can tell when you are faking.

The literature tells us that the leader's job is to provide a vision for the enterprise. When we have a vision, it is what we hope the enterprise to be in the future time – three to five years from a starting point. People in the organization, understanding the vision, will feel more comfortable making decisions. They can decide because they know when their decision supports the vision. This affords the leader an opportunity to give words of encouragement, whenever a subordinate makes the right decision.

Encouragement is a key tool for the leader. By encouraging others a leader gives them the incentive to do more. Leaders are watched by their people. Some are encouraged by the actions of the leader. When the leader takes reasonable risks, the subordinate knows that it is all right for others to take reasonable risks. When the leader strives for perfection, the subordinate knows that excellence is expected and is encouraged to do everything in an excellent manner. We are an example for our people.

As we go so go the people in the organization. When we support and encourage them, they support our goals, mission and vision for the organization. Someone once said that we teach as we were taught. This means we were encouraged by the demeanor and expertise of our teacher. We were impressed and emulated, to the best or our remembrance, by their actions and deeds that encouraged us.

"We can only be what we can see!" Our very being, as leaders, encourages others. Be what we want our people to be.

"You never know when you lift another person with a good word. Always have a good word." David M. Hall

VI

Flexible

"The issue is how do you get old thoughts out of your mind"

As the hurricanes and tornadoes pass through the southeast each fall, it becomes evident that flexibility is a requirement during that season. The trees many times bend and sway, but they do not break. The weaker ones are uprooted and moved by the terrific winds. It takes a mighty strong tree to withstand the winds of hurricanes and tornadoes.

Likewise, as leaders, we will have the winds of change come at us in the workplace. Sometimes these winds are mild. The change is probably sufficiently small and insignificant that the change is not an issue. Some changes, if not made will be of no consequence. People normally accept these types of changes as necessary to doing business and making progress. Their implementation is normally inconvenient but painless. People display their flexibility by listening to others, considering their suggestions or ideas and sometimes accommodating them.

Then there are the winds of changes that completely disturb every facet of a person's current equilibrium. These are the changes that upset the workforce. Imagine the initial conversions from manual records to computer recordkeeping. People were encouraged to go from pencil and paper records, where they could trace their workflow and ascertain errors or the location of errors if the need arose. From this to a machine that held all of their records. No manual audit trail was available. They went from a culture that emphasized correct output to a culture where correct and adequate input became more important than output.

Not only do you change the process, you also need to change the mindset. Changing the process is easy, when you have people who are accustomed to doing what they are told and have no need to take any responsibility. In this day and age where leaders are trying to get people to be accountable and take ownership of the process, the people need to know the reasons for change and to understand the benefits before they see them. Knowing and accepting the reason is what causes people to be flexible and to accept the unknown.

We all make plans for some part of our future. Planning requires that we determine our desired destination on this journey. Once decided, the leader must then devise a plan to get there. A plan is a document that guides one to a destination – goal. A plan requires that we have milestones and checkpoints. These are places along the way where we stop and assess where we are, and determine if we are still on track. We also look at our timing and our resources to see if they have conformed to the plan. Anything out of "sync" at these milestones are reviewed and corrected.

A plan also requires that we have an alternate plan (sometimes called Plan B). No matter how good the plan is, it may not succeed. This does not indicate a failure on the part of the plan, but it does indicate the need for leaders to be both attentive and flexible.

Plans sometimes go awry. When we create plans, leaders need to have alternate plans in event the original plan runs into obstacles along the way. Most obstacles can be overcome. There are times when obstacles pose a challenge that is too great or that was not anticipated. In this instance the alternate plan is helpful.

Planning gives us an opportunity to look at alternatives that help us to select the best way to achieve our goal. When we encounter obstacles, most of them have been considered in the planning process. For those few obstacles that were not considered, we still have alternative goals that we can pursue, because of the planning process. The wind that blows the change is not devastating to the leader who plans. Plans permit the leader to be more flexible and more accommodating of creative and innovative ideas in the marketplace.

"He who fails to plan, plans to fail."
Dwight David Eisenhower

VII

Growth

"If opportunity doesn't knock, build a door." Milton Berle

When we are young we understand growth better. As parents we want our children to grow. We discuss their possible height and weight and size. We also discuss their mental growth. We help them with their homework and we even devise exercises that test their cognitive skills. It is our desire that our children grow physically, mentally, emotionally, socially and even spiritually.

We are normally in our middle years when our children are young. That is a period when most of us are trying to grow on our jobs and in our careers. Each is trying to reach the next rung on the ladder of success. It is natural, I think, for people to want to grow in some part or phase of their lives.

As leaders, we have a responsibility to help the people in our organizations to grow. Their growth makes them a better, more knowledgeable person. It also makes the organization more efficient and creative. So we must grow as we continue to work. In this way we keep abreast of new technology, new techniques and new opportunities that can help us in the workplace and make the enterprise more efficient.

Helping others to grow, avoids a possible void in an organization. Should the leader become ill or incapacitated for an extended period of time, there needs to be someone to do his/her work without major disruption to the organization. At the working level, whenever someone is unable to come to work, there is usually a sharing of that person's responsibilities until the person returns or a replacement is found. At the management level that is not always the case. Too many managers do not train anyone to do their work, so that things can continue to get done in his/her absence.

All things considered, we leaders and managers are hired to get the work done. One way of growing a person is to select the best of your organization and teach him/her elements of your job. Each one learns a different element. When you are absent, your job can be accomplished by the subordinates who have learned the details of what you do. This is one form of secession planning. Secession planning is a responsibility of leadership.

Another approach would be to select someone to mentor. This means you would help this individual to better understand the big picture of your job and your organization. The mentee gains new insights. The mentee understands better the organization and how it fits into the larger organization and the industry.

There are two types of mentors. There is the covert mentor who insures that a particular individual has all of the right opportunities. The covert mentor never identifies him/herself to the mentee. This mentor simply assists in the growth of the mentee from a distance, from the back room, and from the meeting room. He/she serves as a champion for the mentee without the mentee knowing it.

The other type of mentor is the overt mentor. In many instances the mentee has asked a person to serve as his mentor and the mentor agreed. In some cases the mentor selects a person with potential and decides to mentor him/her and help him/her grow in the organization and in the industry.

The leader is hired to make an organization successful and competitive. A part of doing that requires that we do nothing to hinder or slow the processes that need to be impacted daily, weekly, and monthly. We, as leaders, have a responsibility to help people in our organization and in our company to grow. This benefits the person, the manager, the leader and the company.

"You cannot help others without helping yourself". Anonymous

VIII

Honesty

"Sports do not build character. They reveal it." Haywood Brown

Being honest and a person of integrity are not easy. There are too many people who have their own definitions of what it means to be honest. These views sometimes distort how a person looks at a situation. It also causes friends, associates and youth to be confused about the true meaning of honesty.

I will always be honest.

When it is time to alert and update my supervisors or leaders, I will tell them what I think they need to know to make their decision. I am, in effect, passing judgment on their ability to handle more information. I am also deciding for them what it takes, from an information perspective, to make their decision. This could leave them at a disadvantage and cause them to make the wrong decision.

I will always be honest.

Many messages come with good or bad news. Sometimes there is both good and bad news in the same situation that needs to be communicated. Many people will tell the good news with great enthusiasm and joy. They omit the bad news altogether. If someone mentions the possibility of the bad, they manage to soften the bad with comments like, "We are a long way from a decision on that issue." "We have not looked at that issue in the appropriate depth. As soon as we do we will advise you!" When we do this we are not giving our leadership the total picture. We are not giving them the big picture. We feed them pabulum and they think they have sugar.

I will always be honest.

We give the negative a positive spin. We emphasize the positive so that the negative seems minute or of less importance. "No we did not meet the production schedule, but the quality is superb." The person then launches into a diatribe that emphasizes quality, its importance and how the customer is impressed with the great improvement in quality. This is ignoring the problem of adequate production. This is highlighting the positive while minimizing the negative. This leaves the leader feeling good, when the leader should be concerned.

I will always be honest.

Sometimes the leader is the problem when it comes to honesty. Take the case of a leader who asks a manager to give an elevated rating to one of his employees, because of the interest at the leadership level in the organization. The manager has every right to be honest and evaluate a person based on meeting standards and the accomplishment of goals. To use any other criteria is being dishonest.

I will always be honest.

Another tactic by some people is to exclude specific individuals from access to certain information. The holder of the information is in effect making a decision for the other person. The person with the information decides that a certain person should be excluded from receiving certain information, even though the information may have an impact on the person's work or work effort. It is important to insure that every person who is impacted be aware of any and all information that could impact them.

I will always be honest.

We have all seen these and other instances of dishonesty in the workplace. We should work to eliminate these and other forms of dishonesty in all that we do and not tolerate it in those who work with us and for us.

"Being honest with others is easier when we
are honest with ourselves." Anonymous

IX

Innovation

"If at first you don't succeed, try something else." Anonymous

Innovation abounds in the world today. Technology has permitted men/women and organizations to do things that were thought impossible years ago. In the 1940's there were no jet airplanes. Television was to be a reality of the future and these things called personal computers were not even a dream. Actually the computer nerds were trying to figure out a way to create a super computer capable of multiprocessing and complicated computations. Today everything they dreamed of is available on a personal computer in most of the homes in the country. Innovation made it all possible.

Thanks to these and other innovative ideas, people are able to produce more in less time and with fewer people. This portends to be a problem for the nation. Not only does it create unemployment, it also requires people to reorient their thinking and learn new technology and skills. By so doing people remain employed and also keep up with the changes in technology that we inevitably will experience.

Innovation has not been even across the board in every discipline. Some areas have enjoyed more and craftier technology and innovation than others. The field of information technology has had the biggest change. There was a time when a professional in the field of information technology had to learn every aspect of the business. Today the average person is a specialist in only one area – two at the most. Finance and administration has enjoyed many changes, all of which tended to increase productivity. Information technology is gaining a stronger foothold in the health care industry than it has enjoyed before. Computer chips and magnets are helping to increase the innovation in this area.

Manufacturing has enjoyed many improvements from innovation and technology, health care and administrative changes have not kept up with other areas. Much research continues to be performed in this area. Clearly, one day there will be a tremendous break through.

Innovation requires an environment that supports research and development. It requires a mentality that does not penalize people who fail at some idea that could prove to be beneficial if developed. Leaders tend to worry about making as much money as possible in the current environment. The future can only be secured when money is devoted to the future. Some companies reward people who try, even though they may fail. There are, I am sure, many failures in these types of companies, but the one success makes up for the failures. There is a story that some years ago a person in Research and Development at IBM had spent considerable funds trying to develop a newer faster memory. During the first test, the new memory was an abject failure. The employee was disappointed and upset. Later he had to face the president of the company. The employee imagined that he was about to be fired. The president instead of firing the employee acknowledged that about $1 million had been invested in his education. The employee was admonished to go back to work and complete his assigned task.

Leaders should realize that there is nothing guaranteed in the world of innovation. People should be encouraged to try things. If their ideas work, then the organization will benefit. If they don't work, you at least have an employee who is devoted to trying something new. Eventually they will produce something – product or service – that will pay off for the corporation. Creativity should be encouraged. All new inventions have been created by people who thought "outside the box" and wanted to try something new and different.

If the past is any key, the future will produce more innovation. The new innovation will be produced faster than it was in the past. Today, there are more tools available to help innovators do new and different things. What will the future hold? No one knows. Whatever the future holds, it will be full of things that make life more convenient, more productive, and healthier. It will all be due to the innovative thinking of a few people focused on a specific area. That's the way it has always been. It will probably always be that way.

"There is only one corner of the universe you can be certain of improving, and that's your own self." Aldous Huxley

X

Jolt

"One of the rarest things that a man ever does is to do the best he can." Josh Billings

Sometimes people get into a rut. They are accustomed to doing their job in a particular way. They know it well and can do it with ease, speed and efficiency. Then along comes technology. Some people, of necessity, need to be jolted from their position of comfort in an effort to get even greater efficiency. In other words, they need what Robert Massey calls "a significant emotional event."

To get people to buy into doing things differently, and hopefully better, leaders have to give them reasons that the person can also buy into. This can be a jolt to many people because it takes them out of their comfort zone. This jolt must be made using our influence. We need to convince the person of the importance of change. In addition we must show them the value to the company and to them personally.

When you see people with greater potential, they are usually happy doing what they do or they do not wish to up set the normalcy of operation by suggesting that they have a better opportunity. Sometimes people do not realize that they have greater potential. It may take a jolt to convince people to assume the responsibility of improving themselves. Sometimes the improvement can be done by the company and sometimes it must be done by the individual. For the people to have a positive response to improving themselves, they must believe that they can improve and have greater potential. This jolt is the responsibility of the leader.

We live in a competitive world today. Competition abounds from all over. In order for a company to continue to be competitive, it must do more with less. Only so much can be attained by squeezing the suppliers for lower pricing. Eventually, the company must increase its production with what is available to it. Technology is one route to accomplishing increased production. After technology has been explored, it is time to convince each person to contribute to improved production. This can be done in teams or individually. Each person, whether on a team or operating independently, must contribute to improved production. Leaders have a difficult job trying to cause a person to increase his/her production. It is a must if the company is to grow and thrive in a competitive marketplace.

Each employee commands a certain amount of knowledge about the unit in which he/she works. They also have knowledge of the company, the competition and the industry. The more we know the better we can contribute to the success of the organization. Each employee should know and understand the vision and the mission of the organization. Moreover each person must spend time learning more and more about the organization, the industry and the competition. By expanding the knowledge horizon of each individual, we contribute to the production, quality and excellence of the product and the process.

Many times, due to circumstances, it is necessary to have an individual learn a different job. Such changes are for the benefit of the company. It takes the persons out of their comfort zone and places them, many times, in an environment where they operate as a beginner. When this is necessary, we need to select a person who is worthy of the opportunity. That would be someone who has the potential for bigger and better things in the organization. At other times, it becomes important that we ask a person to do more than is normally required or desired of them. It may be due to the absence of another individual or it may be to complete a temporary operational surge. When either of these instances occur, the leader is again in a position where he must use his influence to get the employee to respond favorably.

In each of these instances, the encouragement should be done in private, one-on-one. The leader needs to well prepare himself or herself so that things go as smoothly as possible. Emphasis should be placed on the benefits to the company and the benefits to the individual. When employees understand the benefits, the likelihood of success, in influencing others, increases tremendously.

"Encouragement after censure is as the
sun after a shower." Goethe

XI

Knowledge

"Help with deeds, not with words." Erasmus

As a young man growing up, my grandmother would always tell me and my brother, "Get an education. No one can take that away from you!" The message was that education was the key to whatever we wanted to do. Not a bad thought for a lady who attended school infrequently and for only a few years.

This very thought suggested that we had to know things. If we look at the word knowledge it begins with the word know. This would suggest that knowing things is important. In the business world there are several areas of knowledge that a person must know in order to be successful.

Know your job. We all have a tendency to think that we are good at our jobs. We probably are. There are at least a dozen people capable of doing your job. Many of that dozen are in the same organization with you. So, you must know a bit more than just your job. You must bring something extra, special or value added to the job. In this way you are appreciated for your contributions and the world feels that you really, really know your job.

Know your bosses job: From time to time the boss needs to be away. He/she likes to feel that the place can run smoothly in his/her absence. Each time the boss is going to be away, ask, "What can I do for you while you are away?" Any assignment he/she gives will help you learn the bosses' job. The more you learn the more he/she will depend on you. The more he/she depends on you the more likely you are to be recommended for a job of greater responsibility. You get selected for promotion for both what you do and the potential you show for greater responsibility. You show that potential by asking for more responsibility and doing it well.

Know the business. You represent the business or company twenty-four hours a day. Whenever you are in the community, you are a representative of the business. You must therefore, know the business, and all of its products. You never know when someone will ask you about the company or its products. How does it sound when an employee does not know what is happening in their own company?

Know the industry. Every industry survives because of the people in the industry. Industries get involved in lobbying. They sponsor youth programs to get young people interested in a career in their industry. They advance the use of technology in the industry and they perform studies to help the industry identify problems and improve their processes and their product/service. One must be knowledgeable in these things.

Know people. Building relationships with people in the same business that you are in can be profitable. You can learn from them. You have someone you can call, with whom you can consult – free. If you know the people in your organization, they will better respond to your request for their support. You also need to know who is best at what job or project.

Know something about a potpourri of subjects. Have you ever seen a person who is versed in only one subject? There are many people who can talk only about their job or their career. They are not well versed in a variety of subjects. These people are booooor-ring. Don't be boring. Have a general knowledge about a variety of subjects so that you can have a conversation about something other than work and your career. You are then considered a well rounded person.

Knowledge is the key. Know your job, the organization and the industry. Your knowledge of people can enhance your leadership skills. A well rounded person has the ability to talk about a variety of subjects comfortably. All of these things help a person to be a better leader and manager.

"A little knowledge is a dangerous thing." Anonymous

XII

Learning

"Take advantage of every opportunity; where there is none, make it for yourself." Marcus Garvey

Change happens far too frequently in the marketplace today. The challenge for leadership is to keep up with the change. It is important that new technology and new processes be analyzed and used for the advantage of the enterprise. Competition is fierce today. Companies and organizations and people are continually trying to find new methods to reduce costs and improve the productivity in the workplace.

In view of these and other phenomena, leaders must create a learning environment. Organizations today need an environment where the worker is continually learning and has a desire to learn and apply new knowledge to the processes and policies of the workplace.

Let's look at a few ways that the employees and the managers can keep abreast of the new technology that is available to enable the organization to be more competitive.

1. I know of one organization that assigned a business book to the leadership staff each month. Each month a leader in the organization would review the book at a staff meeting with the managers. The book would be discussed and the managers would be challenged to use some of the principles in the organization to help improve the organization. In addition, at the monthly meetings of the entire organization, the book was reviewed again to everyone in the organization. There was no discussion at the 'Town Hall" meetings, but there was

exposure. This gave everyone in the organization exposure to twelve business books each year.

2. A variation of this same theme is to have a manager read and summarize a business book. Discussion would take place among the management staff. Also the summary would be disseminated throughout the organization. Everyone in the organization had exposure to the book, each month. Each manager would read and summarize two books per year. One would be selected from a Business Books Best Seller List and the other would be selected by the manager.

3. There are companies that sell "Books on Tape" or "Book Summaries." A leader could purchase a subscription for each manager. Managers could listen to the Books on Tape (or CD) daily going to and from work. Because listening is involved, it is easier to listen to the tape or CD over and over again. This helps the person remember the information. Book Summaries are usually one to 5 pages. It does not take long to read and it highlights the most important points of the book. By not reading the book itself, one loses many of the examples and nuances, but the summary captures the salient points.

4. Occasionally it is important to send an employee away from the workplace to attend school, some class or a seminar. Too often, the completion of the course is recorded in the personnel files of the person and that is the end of the discussion on that training. What leaders need to do is require each trainee to devise a plan to use what they have learned while away at school attending some class course or seminar. Leaders should insure that there is some payoff for all the training that the company provides.

5. Because technology changes quickly, many companies engage in a "train the trainer" program. One person goes to a course and returns to train all of the other workers who need that

knowledge. In this way more people are trained without a significant training expense.

6. In some instances, workers will need to pay for their own training. By so doing the worker is investing in himself. The worker is more likely to be considered for promotion and will be more competitive in the marketplace.

Training is important. Continuous training is essential for the individual and the organization. Training moves both the individual and the organization to the next level. Often it can be the training of the employees that makes the difference. Creating a learning environment is the answer. When people want to learn, they will find a way to use their new knowledge.

"Stretch your mind and fly." Whitney Young Jr.

XIII

Meaningful Change

"The only person who likes being changed is a wet baby."
Anonymous

Change is inevitable. All organizations must deal with change. Change occurs everyday. Most organizations fall into one of three categories, when it comes to change.

The first category is an organization which does not visualize the need for change. Think about what happens if there is no need for change. Quality and cost are not issues, and the organization sees itself in a rather stable environment. This clearly means that the status quo continues. If this had been the attitude of the automotive industry, we would all be driving Model T's. Organizations today that do not change are not standing still, they are falling behind.

The second category is an organization experiencing incremental changes. These organizations go through a series of small changes. They can always see "the light at the end of the tunnel" and it is a bright light. This requires leadership to be organized. It requires some preplanning so that the changes are made in the right order and at the right time to take full advantage of the benefits of the change.

The third category is an organization that initiates multiple changes at a rapid pace. This, many times, drives people to chaos when they have to deal with multiple changes. Which action belongs to what change? When a solution comes, it is difficult to identify which change caused the solution. This opens the organization up to new and different problems. Who takes the credit, if the change is good? Who do we blame if the change did not turn out to accomplish its objective?

Ideally, we should try to be an organization in the second category. This is the essence of continuous improvement: to make small meaningful changes that are well paced so that results are evident in the short term. Also the likelihood of the change having long term impact is better. This process is less upsetting to the people. The process also is easier to effect. This process is destined to have greater buy-in from the people. Change is easier when the people understand the reason for the change and can see a benefit to their job and to them personally.

Change is happening faster than ever before. If we measure the rate of difference of time between the submission and the required implementation of a required change, we will find that the allotted time per request is decreasing. Therefore, the pace of change is accelerating. This trend points to the need for multiple, small, manageable change rather than large, comprehensive change.

To prevent the dysfunctional behavior brought on by change, described by Alvin Toffler in his book *Future Shock* we need to avoid complex, high volume, fast-paced change. To be successful, we must bring on change through what W. Edwards Deming calls "continuous improvement."

"The only thing certain is change." Anonymous

XIV

Negotiations

"You don't get what you deserve, you get what you negotiate."
Anonymous

Every interchange between people is a negotiating session. Most interchanges are to inform. Sometimes they are to persuade or to sell a product or idea. There are other communications interchanges and they are all engaged in the negotiating process. In each instance the message sender is trying to educate, inform or persuade the communications receiver. It is not an easy task.

Stephen Covey in his book, *Seven Habits of Highly Effective People*, admonishes us to adopt a win-win philosophy. This suggests that in a negotiating session there will be two winners. Each side will get what he/she wants. In order to affect a win-win result, each side must listen carefully to the other side to ascertain exactly what he/she wants and the reasons for wanting it. When we listen, we may find that we are not as far apart as we suspect. Listening is the key to understanding. Understanding is the key to helping others get what they want while we get what we want. To do this we must be creative. We must also be genuine.

Covey cautions against having a win-lose philosophy or a lose-win philosophy. In the win-lose philosophy, we cause the other person to lose. This makes them opponents. Causing someone to lose in a sporting event or game is the proper thing to do. Causing a person to lose in the marketplace or in the organization is not the thing to do. This action can cause resentment, anger, frustration and disappointment. It is important that we abandon the win-lose philosophy, in business, Win-lose causes everyone to lose, because it causes distrust.

Lose-win is the philosophy that causes people to give up without a fight. Lose-win says. "I lose, you win." When people perpetually give in they are trying to avoid conflict and turmoil. Conflict and turmoil cannot be avoided. These two things must be dealt with and the sooner the better, in most instances. To constantly give in suggests a weak person, or a person who does not care. In either instance this is not a characteristic to have in anyone on the team. People are respected for gracefully speaking up and offering an opinion or idea that has a chance to improve the organization or resolve issues that exist.

There is one negotiating strategy that should be adopted along with the win-win philosophy. That is what I call the Olympic win negotiating strategy. When Debbie Thomas skated in the Olympics she was forecasted to be the winner. However, she lost by a slim margin. When asked how it felt to be beaten by a virtual unknown, she gave an Olympic answer. She said that she felt good because she had skated better that day than she had ever skated before. Clearly Debbie Thomas was in the business to do her best.

In a separate Olympic event, the downhill ski competition was down to the final two. The first person skied gracefully and almost flawlessly. When skier number one finished, he approached his opponent (Skier number 2) and advised him of things he could do to improve his performance. Skier number two took the advice to heart and managed to beat skier number one by a slim margin.

These two stories are at the heart of the Olympic win. It is important that we each do our best and at the same time help others to do their best.

The win-win philosophy, though difficult to attain, is a must in negotiating in the business world. Moreover the Olympic win is one that we each should personally adopt because it permits us to add value to the organization and insures that we are making our best contribution.

> *"Every conversation has the potential for being the beginning of a negotiation." David M. Hall*

XV

Options

"Successful people consider all of the options."

Someone once said, "There is more than one way to skin a cat." Not only is this true, there is more than one way to do anything that has to be done. This poses a couple of questions. How do we know if we have considered all of the ways to do what we are trying to do? How do we know if we are making the right decision after we have considered the alternatives known to us? The answer is, we don't always know. But we must work at considering as many options as possible.

We need to get the opinions of others before we make a decision. The most important people to offer an opinion are those who will be impacted by the decision. Some leaders feel that their success is because they have been great decision makers. They are probably right, but they forget that they had input and opinions from a host of peers and others before making their decision.

Leaders, many times, have people working for them who will agree with everything they say or decide to do. When the leader has a group of "yes" men or women, he/she is without help. It is the person with the divergent opinion that causes the leader to think, and reconsider his/her position. This reconsideration could lead to other options and a better decision. Unsolicited opinions of others have been known to make some leaders and managers angry. These are closed minded leaders who do not have the advantage of considering all of the available options.

Different options represent opportunity for the leadership in an organization. Some options presented by the workforce can represent a new idea not directly related to the decision requirement being considered at the moment. The important thing is for the leader to create an environment where the people feel that it is safe and healthy to voice their opinion without retribution.

Sometimes when canvassing the opinions and options of the people, the responses will come back with the same recommendation. This means the answer is obvious. This does not indicate a group of "yes" men or women, it simply means in some instances the proper response or decision is obvious. This is often true when a plan is in place for the enterprise or the work unit and people, being aware of the goals, will likely recommend the same decision.

On occasion, even with goals in place and understood, there may be a person who would want to recommend something that is not obvious to all of the others contributing input. In most instances this person is looked upon as someone who has a personal or private agenda. Actually this person is our best friend. Because of his/her differing opinion, we have a chance to learn something new or to further educate the person who has the different opinion of what should be done.

History has shown that the more input we have the more likely we are to make the right decision. This tells us that we need to garner as much input as possible from as many sources as possible so that we, as a leader, are as informed as our people. This improves tremendously the odds of the leader making the most efficient decision for the issue at hand.

"All good decision-making requires input from multiple sources."

XVI

Preparing a Leader

"Be ye' ever ready." Author unknown

Every business has a desire to stay in business. It is rare, if ever, when you meet a business man or woman who indicates that his/her goal is to go out of business. An essential ingredient to the successful business is a secession plan. This requires every person to insure that there is someone to replace them if they are unavailable to work. The higher the level in the organization the more important it is to have a secession plan. The responsibility for finding a successor rests with the leaders themselves.

Leaders need to get to know their people and their talents well enough that they can identify a person or persons who have the talent and desire to replace them. To some leaders this can be threatening. Leaders must get past these threats. Leaders have a responsibility for the smooth operation of the enterprise.

No one wishes a leader bad luck, but there is always the possibility that he or she may not be able to work or to perform his/her duties at some point in time. It is always prudent to identify someone and mentor and train them in event of the leaders' unavailability. The leader should select a person or persons who have potential and gradually give them more responsibility.

Another approach, that works well, is to give the mentees a hypothetical or a real case and ask what action should be taken. This gives them a chance to test their decision-making skills. It also gives you, the leader, the opportunity to discus their decision and to coach them in the decision-making process.

When leaders find associates with leadership potential, in addition to mentoring them, they should also be a coach. Coaching takes care of the here and now. Coaching is a tool used to help associates improve in whatever they are doing at the moment. Coaching gets close to telling a person how to do something. It is important, in the process, that all details be given. More important, it is to get the associate over a particular hurdle or to show them a way to improve a process in which they are engaged.

Another part of preparing leaders is to keep them well trained. In this age of technological change, we need to keep people abreast of all new tools that can assist them in their work. The idea is to make each person the best that they can be and to continue to assist them in improving whatever he/she is doing. We use the expression "continuous improvement" often times when discussing the processes on the plant floor. We also need to think in terms of our human capital, in the organization, and insure that there is also continuous improvement. People need to have their skills and knowledge upgraded on a regular basis. In this way they can use their skills to assist the enterprise to become more efficient.

It is also the responsibility of the leader to set a great example. People tend to imitate their leaders. This being the case, people need to see great leadership in order to be great leaders. What ever works for you, as a leader, your associates are apt to try and see if it will work for them. This is one way in which people grow. This is an important way of preparing potential leaders.

Preparing leaders is an awesome responsibility. It is necessary in every enterprise. It is the glue that holds an organization together when a part of the organization is missing for a period of time. It is also the way that people become qualified and eventually reach the next level in the organization.

Many leaders fear that if they train people too well, they will leave the enterprise and join a new company. That is certainly a risk. However, the positive side of that action is that you have a person in another company whom you trained, and feels a bit of loyalty to you. You can even team up with that person to exchange ideas and to help you keep abreast of newer technology.

When you prepare a person to replace you, you have the potential for greater efficiency in the organization. Efficiency is one of the main duties of the leader.

"You can't be what you can't see" Author unknown

XVII

Quitting:
is not an option.

"Never quit. Find a different way to succeed." David M. Hall

General Daniel "Chappie" James, the first black four star general in the United States Air Force loved to tell stories about his mother. Once he told the story of how his mother, a school teacher, would require her children to memorize things. She felt it improved and developed the mind. "Chappie" was required to memorize the Ten Commandments. With the guidance of his mother a commandment was added. He had to learn Eleven Commandments. Commandment number eleven was, **"I shall not quit."**

As we go through life, each of us takes on things that challenge us. We can quit or we can adopt the philosophy of Mrs. James, and declare no matter what,

I shall not quit.

The world is full of naysayers. All of us interface with them as we go through life. These are the people who tell us that our idea will not work. They may indicate that they tried it once and it did not work for them. They give you no encouragement and see no possibility of your success, regardless of your approach. To these naysayers, you should say:

I will not quit.

In the workplace today, it is the current philosophy of modern management that all of the people in the organization should know the vision and mission of the organization. There are those who would exclude you from this knowledge. They are from the old school of management. They feel that certain knowledge is the province of a certain level of people. This leaves you with a void in your knowledge of the organization and may cause you to make decisions not in concert with the vision and mission of the organization. In spite of this, you should say:

I will not quit.

We all have our standards for ourselves and for our coworkers. We use these standards to judge ourselves and our coworkers. If they measure up to our standards, they are a good worker. If they do not measure up, they are a worker less competent than us and a person who needs training or motivation. Many times we see others getting away with producing less than the standard. If they can get away with it, why not us? Too many of us will slack off and do less than we are capable. In a sense it is a form of quitting because you are producing less than your capability. You should not get caught in that trap. Your standards should me met. Your attitude should be:

I will not quit.

These are but a few of the examples of different things that can cause us to quit, give up and move on to something easier. There is nothing that says or requires life, the job, marriage or any other relationship to be easy. There will always be tough times. It takes a tough person to meet tough times. Toughness requires us to regularly repeat to ourselves, the phrase:

I will not quit.

Quitting was not an option in the James household. Once you started something, you had to see it through. If you were successful, there were lessons to be learned. If you were a failure, there were lessons to be learned. Her philosophy was that quitting does not permit one to learn from the experience. We would all do well to adopt that philosophy.

I will not quit.

"If you plan to quit, you should not have started." David M. Hall

XVIII

Risk-taking

"There is some risk in all that we do!"

Risk is the process of trying something for the first time. When we do that we are not sure of the outcome. We are not sure of the consequences. We take the risk because we believe that there is something better to be gained for either ourselves or the enterprise.

Risk is different for everyone. Risk is based on training, education and experience. For a person who has been exposed to something, trying something new is not as great a risk as a person who has not had the exposure. Driving a car at 120 miles an hour, on a freeway, is a great risk for a person who uses his car only for work and an occasional annual trip. That same speed for a professional race car driver, on a race track, would probably seem a bit slow.

There are degrees of risk also that must be considered. We are told that investing money is risky, but some risks are greater than others. Investing in bonds with the federal government appears to have low risk. Investing that same money with the card tables in Las Vegas, Nevada would have a far greater risk. There are several risk options in between. There is no option that is completely without risk. If we put our money under the mattress, we are still at risk. The house may catch fire or someone may steal the money. Taking risks is important and we all do it. The important thing is to not gamble. Always take calculated risk. These are risks where we have an opportunity to prosper.

People who take risks are the people who are creative and innovative and have the security to try that which is new and different. In the marketplace, it is the person who takes the risk that helps move the organization to the next level. We must remember that all risks do not end in great reward. Some risks that are taken have dire consequences. Some are only partially successful. Others move us or the organization to a higher level.

Some people do not take risks, or they take small risks. Many people refuse to take risks because they cannot see the consequences and they fear the consequences are greater than they desire to bear. Procrastination causes some to not take risks. These people wait until they have all the facts and all of the answers before they start anything. Because of this, they never get started. If they do, their beginning is too late and of no consequence, because someone else has already done it or it is no longer significant to do. There are people who simply do not like change. These people not only do not like risk, but they prefer the status quo. Negative people avoid risk. They would prefer to analyze and assess the actions and creative efforts of others than get involved in any creative activity of their own.

Conversely, there are those who have an affinity to risk. They believe that there is a level of risk that everyone can tolerate. They find their level and they take risks that fall within that tolerance level. In addition, these risk takers have a tendency to occasionally stretch their risk tolerance. This means they go past their normal level of tolerance and try for a little greater risk. These risk takers normally do things in increments. Each risk they take becomes a little more risky each time. In addition, when a large project is involved, they will divide the project into milestones and work diligently to keep abreast of the risks involved.

People, who are confident, tend to be the risk takers in the business world. These people normally are positive in their outlook and believe that all will work out, in spite of the naysayers that may surround them. Ambitious people who are interested in climbing the corporate ladder as swiftly as possible tend to be risk takers. People have difficulty moving up the ladder of success without taking some risk that benefits the enterprise.

Risk takers are generally forward thinking people. They have a vision of what could be better and they are willing to try it. One success leads to another and they keep taking risks. Success is looked upon as an experience that gives us lessons that are important to remember when a person takes the next risk.

There is probably some level of risk in all that we do. Some risk we can tolerate. This is a low level of risk. Some risk causes us to have heart palpitations. These mid level risks keep us mentally alert and healthy. The high level risk can be downright scary. Either way, there is risk in almost all that we do. If there is no risk an enterprise is stagnant.

> *"If there is no risk there is no progress!"*
> *Author unknown*

IX

Servant

"To serve is to lead." Author unknown

In a discussion with a colleague, it was brought to my attention that the word "service" is defined in the dictionary as "an act of assistance." This suggests that to be a servant leader it is our responsibility to assist the people who support us in the achievement of the organizational goals.

I began to assess how I measured up in my acts of assistance. After some deliberation with myself, I decided that I had been the recipient of the good grace of servant leaders.

Some examples:

- When I worked for a leader we will call Max, he told me my responsibilities on the first day. He then tasked me to carry out my assignments and accomplish my goals. He admonished me not to call him unless I was in trouble. Max empowered me to do the job without recourse to him or anyone else.

- As a young man I was selected to be the officer in charge of a conversion of manual records to mechanized records. These were the old days of Punched Card Accounting Machines. We took the manual records and converted them to the old IBM Punched Card Mechanized Format. This was the forerunner to computers, and permitted people to access and update records faster and more accurately. Although I knew nothing about the equipment and the process, I was given a unique opportunity.

- At one point of my career, a new functional manager decided that I was not qualified to hold the job, to which I had been assigned. He pursued my removal. He had a candidate he felt was better qualified. My boss decided that the approach, to relieve me, was wrong. Further he felt that he needed to have records comparing me and the proposed incumbent. Upon examination it was decided that I was far more qualified. As a result, I remained in the job. I received the total support of by supervisor. He took my case to the highest levels of the organization to insure that I remained in the job for which I was qualified.

- My first evaluation with another leader taught me about servant leadership. I expected him to discuss my performance, our relationship, and our goals, among other things. Instead, he began by asking me to evaluate him. How well was he doing his job? What opportunities did he miss? What could he have done better to make my job easier? These are just a few of the questions we discussed for over an hour before we began to talk about me. It was clear to me that he had a burning desire to be a servant leader. He was.

- Every person who left my organization was interviewed by me. These interviews occurred regardless of the person's level in the organization. It did not matter if the person was reassigned, fired, retired, or leaving the organization. From each of these sessions I learned something about the person and something about the organization. It said to people that you cared for the organization and the people who made the organization work.

- When I joined General Motors, the person to whom I reported, made sure that I met all of the people who would be influential in my job. He also insured that I had everything I needed to be successful. His philosophy was, "I hired you, and it is my responsibility to make you successful." This is a great philosophy to have. We should all have this philosophy. If we did, fewer people would fail in the workplace.

These are but a few examples of servant leadership. In order for an organization to be successful, the leader must serve the people who are assigned to him and who make the organization move in the right direction. Can you outline the things you have done to insure that you are a servant leader?

"Service is its own reward." Anonymous

XX

Thanks

"There are two types of people; those who are forgetful and those who say thanks." David M. Hall

Each year the congressman of each state gets to appoint two deserving young people to the military academies. Normally, they appoint a board whose task it is to review the applicants and recommend to the congressman the top two candidates.

These appointments are taken seriously by the young candidates. They are on their best behavior when they interview and they put their best effort into completing their application. Selecting the best is not an easy task.

A few years ago a young high school graduate named Bryce applied to his congressman from the state of Missouri. After reviews and interviews, he was not selected as one of the top two. The candidates are normally notified in the April/May timeframe. He even learned that he was not number three on the list. Although he was disappointed, he understood the process and was happy for the two young men selected.

He discussed with his father his non-selection. They agreed that he should press on with his life and pursue an alternate plan. Young Bryce made arrangements to attend a local college in or near his home town. He recalls that his father gave him a piece of advice that was valuable and has stood him in good stead through the years. He recommended that Bryce write a "thank you" letter to the congressman. "Why" was a natural response since he was not selected? "Always say thanks," he was admonished.

As fate would have it, during the summer, one of the chosen candidates was involved in an automobile accident. Unfortunately the extent of his injuries would not permit him to attend West Point in the fall. Bryce was unaware of this. Had he been aware it would have been of no consequence to him since he was not the next candidate anyway.

The congressman was approached and advised by one of his staffers about the situation. The staffer recommended that the next person – number three on the list – be given the opportunity to attend West Point. The congressman declined to agree. Instead he said, "Give the appointment to the kid named Bryce. He is the only one to write me a "thank you" letter."

The power of **"Thank you"** is awesome.

Thank you makes people feel good. They know they have done something that is appreciated. Sometimes people try to do something for us and don't succeed, thank them anyway. After all, they did not have to try.

Too often we have loss the habit of saying "please" and "thank you" to other people. If you don't believe me, go to the nearest department store in your local mall, stand near the door and open it for every person who comes in. You will find it is a great day when half of the people express appreciation for your efforts.

Thank you is the oil that eases open the door to people's hearts. Thank you is the salve that decreases a persons desire to shut others out. Thank you is the glue that brings people together with a common understanding of at least one thing – the value of thank you.

Always say, "Thank you" to your people. It will make them feel appreciated and it will make you feel good. Who knows, you just may influence someone else, by your example, to say "thank you."

"Thank you is too often forgotten." Author unknown

XXI

Undeveloped Dreams

"Dreams without action are still dreams." David M. Hall

There is a country and western song that suggests that one should not marry a dreamer. This may not be good advice. Maybe one does want to marry a dreamer. At least the dreamer has an indication of where he/she wants to be at some future time. The dreamer then is to be valued as a planner. The dreamer's plan is in his head. Seldom does he/she share the dream with others. The dreamer cherishes the dream, and looks forward to making the dream a reality one day.

Dreamers are planners. In all of our lives we are forever and perpetually planning. The process of planning causes us to determine where we want to be. We then must develop a process of getting there. The college student enters college with a plan to finish. The college administration assists them with a plan to complete a specific curriculum in the four year time period. Students engage in this plan because they have a dream of what life can and will be like when they achieve their college degree.

Following the plan is developing the dream. This suggests that one must pursue the dream. If the dream is not pursued it remains simply a dream. The dream, then, becomes a goal for the individual. Many of us have dreamed of being wealthy. Some have dreamed of being the leader of some large enterprise. Dreams give us a foundation from which to launch our plan to be successful. Having goals are the key to success. You have something to focus on and work toward.

I am reminded of an airplane trip taken from San Antonio to Dallas. The pilot informed us that there would be turbulence because of the weather in Dallas. This is not a long flight so we flew at a relatively low altitude. As we approached Dallas it was clear that we were into some serious weather. The airplane seemed to drop from our altitude to some lower altitude at a rapid pace. The pilot came on the intercom and advised us that we were enroute to Shreveport, Louisiana.

An essential element of planning is to have a goal. Equally as important is to have an alternate goal. This is what our pilot had. Before pilots take off they are required to file a flight plan that includes their desired destination. In addition, pilots are required to file an alternate goal in event something, like weather, prohibits them from attaining the original goal. The inability to reach a goal can be frustrating and discouraging. That is one of the reasons we have alternate goals. It reduces the level of frustration and gives us an opportunity to take advantage of most of what we have accomplished up to that point.

Many dentists started out in medical school. Many Airplane navigators started in pilot training. For reason we do not know, their original goal was no longer available to them. They did not quit. They did not permit their dream to be unrealized. Instead they took advantage of the knowledge gained, up to that point, and used it to work toward their alternate goal.

Personal goals come from our dreams for ourselves and those close to us. We all should focus on the dreams and develop a plan to accomplish our dreams. When we do we have a better chance to realize our dreams. We leave that lonely, crew of people who spend their lives saying "Could have", "Would have", or "Should have." When we start a process of developing our dreams we avoid that negative language. Undeveloped dreams are, just that, dreams. When we develop a plan for accomplishing our dreams we become the person we are destined to be. Let us develop and pursue our dreams!

"Step one in making your dreams a reality, is getting started."
David M. Hall

XXII

Victim or Victor

"All misfortune is but a stepping stone to fortune."

Henry David Thoreau

We are what we choose to be. It rains on everyone the same. Some choose to complain about the inconvenience of the rain. Their trip is delayed or they suffer the inconvenience of having to carry an umbrella. There are others who look at rain as a good thing. It will improve the look of the grass at my home. The farmers need the rain for the crops. As a result of their efforts we will all eat well.

The same goes for our state of mind. We choose to be victor or victim. It is our choice. No one can make us a victim without our permission. Whether you are victim or victor depends on your point of view.

A shoe salesman was sent to a small country in Africa to develop some sales. The salesman surveyed the situation. After careful analysis of the situation he sent a telegram to his boss at the home office saying, "The people here do not wear shoes. The likelihood of sales is at best, minimum. Request permission to return home?" The salesperson felt he was a victim, being sent to a country to sell shoes where they do not even wear shoes. The salesman was granted permission to return home. A second salesman was posted to the same country. He too surveyed the situation. After careful research he sent the following message to the home office, "No one here wears shoes. Here is lots of potential for high volume sales. Please stand by for large orders of most sizes!"

The difference between these two salesmen is attitude. One chose to be a victim, to be negative. The other chose to be positive. Clearly the positive one has the potential for being the victor. One saw hopelessness, the other saw potential. One was pessimistic, the other was optimistic. Both had the same opportunity.

Another lesson this story teaches us is that there is hope in hopelessness. Nothing is truly hopeless. Hope is an emotion. Hope is an attitude. Hope is an expectation. We all have hope in so many things. Yet there comes a time when things look hopelessness

The victim is the person who has a scarcity philosophy. He feels that when someone else gains something that he/she also wanted that there must be a competition for the item or position or whatever. This philosophy pits one person against another. It causes conflict in an organization. People with this attitude disrupt an organization and do not contribute to teamwork. Actually they prevent teamwork from happening and each person works toward achieving his/her own goals.

The victor is the person who believes that there is enough of everything to go around. He/she believes this is a bountiful country and there is enough of everything for everyone. There is no need to compete for anything. Internal competition can be and sometimes is detrimental to achieving company goals. The victor believes in helping others achieve their goals. By so doing they receive assistance when they are in a quest to achieve their goals. This fosters a team spirit. Not only do the individuals win, but the organization benefits also.

We, and only we, are in a position to choose whether we will be victim or victor. We will either foster a team spirit or we will detract for teambuilding efforts. We either have hope or we believe all is hopeless. We are positive or negative. It is our choice. **Be a victor!**

"A chief is a man who assumes responsibility. He says, 'I was beaten,' he does not say, 'My men were beaten.'" -
- Antoine de Saint-Exupery

XXIII

What Works

"The secret of success is making your vocation your vacation."
Mark Twain

There is much leadership theory being taught in the world today. The theory is good for those trying to learn how to be a leader. Theory will take you only so far. The person for whom you work is not interested in how much theory you know and understand, that manager is interested in how you apply that theory. At some point a person should learn the practical application of leadership. This is what leadership looks for and evaluates. From a practical perspective these are some of the things that work in the world of work.

Model: You are being looked at daily by everyone in the organization. From these, sometimes very brief encounters, opinions are formed about you, who you are and what you believe in. Can a brief encounter be accurate? Probably not, but that does not stop a person from forming an opinion. These opinions, once formed, are oftentimes hard to change. It becomes important then to always be on your best behavior. Let your values show. **"Walk the talk."**

Care: Someone once said, "People don't care how much you know until they know how much you care!" This is sage advice. People are not as impressed with knowledge as they are with how much a person cares. When one thinks about it, there are always an abundance of knowledgeable people. People who really care are less in number. There are many ways to show you care. "Thank you" and "please" show that you, as the leader, respect the individual. Remember a person's name and use it each time you talk to them. Find various ways of giving people a pat on the back for a job well done or for going beyond the requirement or exceeding the standard. The more you can relate to the people in your organization, the more they can relate to you. Be cautious and understand that it is not friendship you seek. Your goal should be to show respect for the individual. Once respect is established, people react differently. There is trust and sometimes even friendship.

Talk to the least of them: Who cleans your office? Do you know their name? Do you know anything about them? The janitor is just as important as your assistant, or deputy. They are both an important part of the team. Know the least of them. Think about the other members of the team and what they think when they see you having a conversation with the janitor. Be assured you are modeling caring behavior. Have a visit with the newest or youngest member of the organization. Make that visit unannounced and at their desk or workplace. Have lunch in the lunchroom with the rank and file employees. Do not always sit with the executives and/or managers. It may upset some middle managers but it will endear you to the people. People like to be acknowledged, remembered and respected at every level of the organization.

Protect your people: When people make a mistake, they usually realize it. They do not need to have you remind them about the error of their ways. What they need is understanding and an effort to help them, by showing them a better way, by securing, for them, additional training or some other show of support. Reprimand is not the answer. You may even ease their fears by telling them of a time when you made a colossal mistake. When the rest of the world is upset by the error, defend them and move on to correct the situation based on a "get well" plan that smells of success.

These are but a few of the things that work successfully for leaders. That is the heart of leadership, how you treat people, and how you take care of people. People are the key to leadership success and enterprise success. They must be treated with respect and dignity at all times and under all circumstances. People make the difference.

"I'd rather be a failure at something I enjoy than be a success at something I hate." George Burns

XXIV

X-Ray

"Everything you do will eventually catch up with you."

When we were small, my brother once said to me, "I think mother has eyes in the back of her head!" She really didn't but it seemed like it because she was able to keep up with what we were doing when we were not in her line of sight. Some of this was intuition, because she knew her sons well.

At other times my mother was able to anticipate what we were going to do and in instances where she disapproved, she would caution us against it. It would appear that she had X-Ray vision – the ability to see inside our head and see and hear what we were about.

Actually there was no X-Ray vision. But she did have an insight into how her sons thought and the environment in which they operated, so that she could anticipate their probable behavior.

We must do the same as leaders in the workplace. Each leader should make some attempt to know well the people for whom he/she is responsible. The leader should also understand the environment. In this way the leader can better understand the people in the organization.

How does one get X-Ray vision? One way is to spend some time talking with the people (one-on-one if possible) so that you understand them, how they think, their concerns on and off the job, and their goals in their career and in life. Although this sounds like a tremendous undertaking, it is a matter of being personable and approachable when engaging people in conversation.

People will share with you if you will share with them. I know a leader who once gathered a segment of his organization together on the last Friday of each month. It was a different group each month. He would discuss with the group the things that worried him, that he was struggling with, and/or the things that kept him awake at night. At some point, some surely worried about his sanity. Managers are not known for their ability to admit that there are things that worry them. It suggests problems that have not been solved. Some managers feel it makes them look weak when they discuss worrisome issues.

The beauty of this session was the result. People began to talk to the leader about options they felt he could use to resolve certain issues. A few had real solutions. All, however, felt a part of the team to the extent that they not only contributed potential solutions, they felt ownership of the unit and the issues. They worked toward being proactive so that new problems could be avoided. IN SHORT, THEY CARED. Leadership could anticipate their actions because of what appeared to be X-Ray vision.

One-on-one sessions with employees are almost mandatory to be a successful leader. Many people do it many ways. It could be catching who ever is at the coffee bar and starting a conversation. It could be the leader sitting down at the desk of an employee to discuss their work assignment and their career. It could be asking someone in the organization to teach you something. There are many more ways of having one-on-one conversation with employees.

Regardless of how you do it, getting to know people past their work association gives you an edge in anticipating how they will react and respond to different situations. In so doing you gain your own version of X-Ray vision that helps you understand people in the organization and they gain an X-Ray vision of you that helps them help you to become successful.

"Everything you do or don't do sends a message." Author unknown

XXV

You

"Tell a person what to do, not how to do it."

A husband and wife were discussing the teen age daughter. It appears the daughter had a momentous (for her) decision to make regarding a school project. The mother explained the project and the dilemma to the father in great detail. She even discussed the emotional state that the daughter was in because of the dilemma she faced. The father listened intently. When his wife finished the father said, "If that were me I would do . . . Moreover, I would not worry about the teacher in this instance. I would just complete the project the best I could and then await the results. If it was me and I did not like it I would appeal to the proper authority." The wife chimed in at this point and exclaimed, "It's not about you!"

As managers and leaders we must remember it is not about us. We had our day, presumably, and it is now the day and time of someone else who is younger and, although we loathe to admit it, smarter. It is not about me and you. It is about the person who is in the trenches doing the work.

Some leaders can't move on. The person gets promoted to a leadership position and they continue to do the work that they were supposed to leave to someone else. By doing this they are indicating that they can't do the work to which they have been assigned. In order to look productive they do the work of others. Dr. Laurence Peter who wrote *The Peter Principle* suggests that this person has reached his/her "peter level." The peter level is the level at which the person is incompetent to do the work. Some companies have trial promotions to test a person before he/she awards them the increased salary and benefits. This is done to see if the person can perform at the higher level.

Some managers stay behind by delving into the "how to" of the person who took their old job. In other words, the manager spends his/her time overseeing the subordinates' job very closely. The supervision is both controlling and stifling. While this is happening there is a manager who is not doing the work they are being paid to do and there is a subordinate who is unhappy because he/she can't do their job without interference.

I attended a retirement celebration for a friend. Several people were asked to speak. One person used the word "I" thirteen times, after I started counting. He spoke for a total of six minutes. He said very little about the retiree, but we all knew his career pedigree. He and the retiree had parallel careers. The "I" suggests that the speech was really about the presenter and not about the retiree.

Many times, in the workplace we use the word "I" too often. We remember how "I" did it when "I" had the job. We discuss with the subordinate what "I" would do if "I" were in the same situation. "I" tends to turn a person off when they are seeking counsel or advice. There is a quote that suggests that when things go wrong is the time for the manager/leader to us the word "I." "We" should be used when things go well and the leader should point to the subordinate when something outstanding has been accomplished.

We should be in the background as leaders. We should insure that the credit goes to the person doing the work. The person should be allowed to make some mistakes and recover and learn his/her own lessons from the mistakes. Leadership is about growing people. We can't grow people by telling them how great we are or how well we did it sometime ago. We grow people by encouraging them. Through encouragement people are destined to improve, under our leadership.

"Train your people and then give them a portion of your power. They will use it wisely." David M. Hall

XXVI

Zap

"Make a difference." Author unknown

Walking along the beach, a man saw someone ahead of him picking up something and throwing it in the water. As he approached the person, he noticed that the person was picking up starfish that had washed up on the beach, and throwing them back into the water. "What are you doing?" he inquired. The man replied that he was trying to save the starfish by throwing them back into the water. "Do you see how many starfish there are out here? You can't possibly make a difference. The man picked up a starfish, threw it into the water and said, "I made a difference to that one."

Each time he zapped a starfish back into the water he made a difference. As leaders we have an opportunity to zap our people and make a difference in their lives. When we zap another person, we give that person somewhat of a shock, a surprise. A proper surprise at the right time can be motivational and inspire a person to continue on in his/her endeavors.

When we pass by a person and praise him/her quietly for something they have done that made a difference, we have zapped that person. The person is surprised. The person is pleased. The person knows that he/she is appreciated. We should never pass up these opportunities. At the same time we should not use these types of compliments for frivolous things. These compliments should be given for things of importance.

You attend a staff meeting or some other organizational meeting and the boss compliments you in front of all of your peers. You will probably be embarrassed. But this type of embarrassment you can stand and understand. It gives your boss an opportunity to recognize those who contribute over and above. It provides recognition for value added contributions. This can be inspirational for others. "If he/she can do it so can I!" could be the attitude of a peer. This type of thing could boomerang and soon everyone is contributing over and above the required standard.

It is said that the sweetest sound to a person is listening to the calling of his/her own name. On meeting someone, most of us forget the name. How impressive it is when someone calls you by name. "They remembered!" you think. This causes you to have a favorable impression of that person. The leader who remembers names is a good leader. Sometimes you may stumble on a name but people forgive you because you tried. If you can't remember the name but can remember a prior conversation of something about a member of their family or their work situation, you have sent an equally good signal that you remember. Remembering means you care.

Unsolicited help is another way of showing that you appreciate a person. When you see a person struggling to do a particular job, it is obvious he/she needs help. When you quietly intervene and assist that person you make a difference in his/her life. Too often we look at the person in need of help and rejoice in the fact that it is not us. Covert action is also a way of helping a person. You give them assistance in discussion with others, without telling them. They benefit from your recommendation and they have no knowledge who recommended them.

Select a person to mentor. This will surprise and may even shock the person. Everyone needs a mentor. Successful people have been mentored at some point in their career. Mentoring helps people in those areas that give the person an edge on others.

To zap is to stun, to surprise. These actions are all actions that are unexpected and unsolicited. They meet the requirement of zapping someone. A positive zap will go a long way in making an employee happy while motivating others to greater heights. Find your starfish and zap them as the person did along the beach.

"Stun the world with your speed and expertise."
Author unknown

Bibliography

Covey, S (1989). <u>Seven habits of highly effective people</u>. New York: Simon & Schuster.

Deming, W. E. (1990). <u>Out of crisis.</u> Cambridge: MIT

If you would like a copy of this book, please complete the form below, and mail to:

Author House
1663 Liberty Drive Suite 200
Bloomington IN 47403

Copies are also available at:

Crimiel Publications LLC
P. O. Box 20061
49 West Hannum Boulevard
Saginaw, MI 48202

Shipping and Handling is $3.00 for the first copy and $2.50 for each additional copy.

Number of copies _____ x $12.99   _____

Shipping and Handling   _____

State Tax   _____

    Total   _____

Thank you for your order. You should receive your order within three weeks.

About The Author

The author is uniquely qualified to discuss the various characteristics of leadership. He has held leadership roles and executive positions in the federal government, corporate America and in several non-profits. He has practiced these and other characteristics throughout his work life and it merited him a degree of success. He shares these characteristics for your education, edification and enjoyment.

Mr. Hall is a graduate of Howard University and The North Carolina Agricultural and Technical State University. He earned his PhD from Kennedy Western University in Business Administration. He is also a graduate at the Advanced Management Program at MIT. During his service in the United States Air Force he attented the Air War College and the Industrial College of the Armed Forces.

Hall began his military career as an airman and retired as a Brigadier General. His awards and decorations are numerous. Upon retirement he was awarded the United States Air Force Distinguished Service Medal. He has also been honored by the Boy Scouts of America. In addition he had received several awards for service to various communities in which he has lived.

He is married to the former Jacqueline Branch of Washington, D.C. From this union there were two sons. The Halls are the proud grandparents of three.

Printed in the United States
141353LV00005B/1/A